The Kingman Comprehension Series

Advanced Level 8

Dr. Alice Kingman

PARTRIDGE

| ISBN: | Softcover | 978-1-5437-7473-3 |
| | eBook | 978-1-5437-7472-6 |

Print information available on the last page.

To order additional copies of this book, contact
Toll Free +65 3165 7531 (Singapore)
Toll Free +60 3 3099 4412 (Malaysia)
orders.singapore@partridgepublishing.com

www.partridgepublishing.com/singapore

Contents

Acknowledgements

First, I would like to thank Jazzy, the illustrator of the Kingman Comprehension Series, for her beautiful artistic drawings which bring every story she has worked on to life.

My great appreciation is also to be extended to my two daughters, Stephanie and Audrey, who helped me from the very beginning in the typing and formatting of questions for every reading passage.

A big thank you to my beloved husband, Matt, for his continuous support, encouragement and professional assistance in the computerised structuring of the book.

I am also grateful to all my students for their contributions to this project, working on different passages, testing out questions and providing invaluable feedback.

With no reservation, my heartfelt gratitude goes to my beloved late father, Joseph, who spared no effort in teaching me English since I was seven years old.

Thank you to all other members of my family who spurred me on to take this big step in realising my dreams of becoming an English-language author. I thank them for their love and patience throughout the whole process. Thank you to my wonderful church family as well for their uplifting prayers and support.

Last but not least, I thank God, my Heavenly Father, every day for His unfailing presence and spiritual guidance, without which this project would not have happened.

To Teacher and Parent

In my lifelong career as an English-language teacher, I have often been disappointed and discouraged to find questions set for comprehension passages stressing speedy location of answers or meticulous reproduction of the text. The formulated questions seldom encourage students to read between the lines or genuinely understand the writer's choice of diction and intention of writing. In other words, students are often deprived of opportunities to think out of the box and explore implied meanings and examine the purpose of sentence structure.

Hence, it has always been my ambition to produce a comprehension series that can sharpen students' skills in analytical discernment. The Kingman Comprehension Series comprises high-interest selections of different literary genres from classics to renowned children's literature including fables, folk and fairy tales, poems, legends, myths as well as modern realistic fictions. It is my hope that students will find the works of the outstanding authors in the books not only enjoyable to work on but also interesting enough to spark further independent reading among themselves.

Daddy-Long-Legs

Jean Webster

When I came to the house on Madison Avenue it looked so big and brown and forbidding that I didn't dare go in, so I walked around the block to get up my courage. But I needn't have been a bit afraid; your butler is such a nice, fatherly old man that he made me feel at home at once. "Is this Miss Abbott?" he said to me, and I said, "Yes," so I didn't have to ask for Mr. Smith after all. He told me to wait in the drawing-room. It was a very <u>somber</u>, magnificent, man's sort of room. I sat down on the edge of a big upholstered chair and kept saying to myself:

"I'm going to see Daddy-Long-Legs! I'm going to see Daddy-Long-Legs!"

Then presently <u>the man</u> came back and asked me please to step up to the library. I was so excited that really and truly my feet would hardly take me up. Outside the door he turned and whispered, "He's been very ill, Miss. This is the first day he's been allowed to sit up. You'll not stay long enough to excite him?" I knew from the way he said it that he loved you—and I think he's an old dear!

Then he knocked and said, "Miss Abbott," and I went in and the door closed behind me.

It was so dim coming in from the brightly lighted hall that for a moment I could scarcely make out anything; then I saw a big easy chair before the fire and a shining tea table with a smaller chair beside it. And I realized that a man was sitting in the big chair propped up by pillows with a rug over his knees. Before I could stop him he rose—sort of shakily—and steadied himself by the back of the chair and just looked at me without a word. And then—and then—I saw it was you! But even with that I didn't understand. I thought Daddy had had you come there to meet me for a surprise.

Then you laughed and held out your hand and said, "Dear little Judy, couldn't you guess that I was Daddy-Long-Legs?"

In an instant it flashed over me. Oh, but I have been stupid! A hundred little things might have told me, if I had had any wits. I wouldn't make a very good detective, would I, Daddy?— Jervie? What must I call you? Just plain Jervie sounds disrespectful, and I can't be disrespectful to you!

Answer the following questions.

1. Judy was very impressed by the house on _____ because it was so _____ and _____.

2. Why did Judy walk around the block before she went into the house?

3. Match the butler with the correct answers:

                      a. looked like a fatherly old man.

                      b. made Judy feel at home at once.

   The butler   c. did not ask Judy for her name.

                      d. cared for Mr. Smith a lot.

                      e. should not be the one to open the door.

4. A synonym for the underlined adjective "sombre" is
   a. inspiring
   b. solemn
   c. cheerful

5. Who is "the man" underlined in the third paragraph referring to?

6. What idiom found in the third paragraph means "I felt weak"?

7. Why did the butler try to suggest to Judy that she should not stay long?

8. When one could scarcely make out anything, one
   a. could not make anything useful.
   b. could not see anything clearly.

9. Why was the man sitting in the big chair propped up by pillows with a rug on his knees?

10. Four caesuras are used in the fifth paragraph to create
    a. shocks
    b. contrasts
    c. dramatic pauses

11. Judy would not call the man "Jervie" because it sounded _____ to her.

12. Which line tells us that truth dawned on Judy all of a sudden?

Read on:

In this last letter written by Judy to Daddy-Long-Legs, we learn that Jervis has finally confessed, after four years, that he is the one Judy has been writing and revealing her most intimate feelings to. The story ends with Judy finally reciprocating her benefactor's true love for her and comes to understand the grand scheme of things that has guided her to where she is now.

Daddy-Long-Legs, written by Jean Webster, is an amazing story about how different moments of our lives can have different meanings for us.

Rip Van Winkle

Washington Irving

On the other side he looked down into a deep mountain glen, wild, lonely, and shagged, the bottom filled with fragments from the impending cliffs, and scarcely lighted by the reflected rays of the setting sun. For some time Rip lay musing on this scene; evening was gradually advancing; the mountains began to throw their long blue shadows over the valleys; he saw that it would be dark long before he could reach the village, and he heaved a heavy sigh when he thought of encountering the terrors of Dame Van Winkle.

As he was about to descend, he heard a voice from a distance, hallooing, "Rip Van Winkle! Rip Van Winkle!" He looked round, but could see nothing but a crow winging its solitary flight across the mountain. He thought his fancy must have deceived him, and turned again to descend, when he heard the same cry ring through the still evening air; "Rip Van Winkle! Rip Van Winkle!"—at the same time Wolf bristled up his back, and giving a low growl, skulked to his master's side, looking fearfully down into the glen. Rip now felt a vague apprehension stealing over him; he looked anxiously in the same direction, and perceived a strange figure slowly toiling up the rocks, and bending under the weight of something he carried on his back. He was surprised to see any human being in this lonely and unfrequented place, but supposing it to be some one of the neighbourhood in need of his assistance, he hastened down to yield it.

On nearer approach he was still more surprised at the singularity of the stranger's appearance. He was a short square-built old fellow, with thick bushy hair, and a grizzled beard. His dress was of the antique Dutch fashion—a cloth jerkin strapped round the waist-several pair of breeches, the outer one of ample volume, decorated with rows of buttons down the sides, and bunches at the knees. He bore on his shoulder a stout keg, that seemed full of liquor, and made signs for Rip to approach and assist him with the load. Though rather shy and distrustful of this new acquaintance, Rip complied with his usual alacrity; and mutually relieving one another, they clambered up a narrow gully, apparently the dry bed of a mountain torrent. As they ascended, Rip every now and then heard long rolling peals, like distant thunder, that seemed to issue out of a deep ravine, or rather cleft, between lofty rocks, toward which their rugged path conducted. He paused for an instant, but supposing it to be the muttering of one of those transient thunder-showers which often take place in mountain heights, he proceeded. Passing through the ravine, they came to a hollow, like a small amphitheatre, surrounded by perpendicular precipices, over the brinks of which impending trees shot their branches, so that you only caught glimpses of the azure sky and the bright evening cloud. During the whole time Rip and his companion had labored on in silence; for though the former marvelled greatly what could be the object of carrying a keg of liquor up this wild mountain, yet there was something strange and incomprehensible about the unknown, that inspired awe and checked familiarity.

Answer the following questions.

1. The adjectives used to describe the deep mountain glen are _____, _____ and _____.

2. The description of "evening gradually advancing" is an example of
    a. a simile
    b. repetition
    c. personification

3. In your own words, say what Rip Van Winkle would be afraid of if he got home late.

4. Which word in the second paragraph suggests that the crow was flying on its own?

5. Underline the part of the sentence in the second paragraph which means "he thought he was fooled by his imagination."

6. Wolf was probably Rip Van Winkle's _____. Explain.

7. How did Rip Van Winkle feel when he heard his name called four times?

8. The strange figure was bending under the weight of something he carried on his back. This implies that the something on his back was:
    a. heavy
    b. elastic
    c. mysterious

9. How do we know Rip Van Winkle was a kind and helpful fellow?

10. True or False:
    a. The stranger's appearance was unique. _____
    b. The stranger was cleanly shaven. _____
    c. The stranger was dressed in an old Danish fashion. _____

11. Did Rip Van Winkle and the stranger talk on the way? How do you know?

12. Arrange the following happenings in the story in the correct sequence:
    _____ Rip Van Winkle heard his name being called.
    _____ Rip Van Winkle walked down the mountain.
    _____ Rip Van Winkle came to a small amphitheatre.
    _____ Rip Van Winkle hastened to help the stranger.

Read on:

Published in 1819 and one of the most famous pieces of writing by Washington Irving, *Rip Van Winkle* depicts a Dutch-American man who has a habit of avoiding useful work. Up in the Catskill Mountains, he encounters some mysterious folks who offer him their strong wine. Rip Van Winkle falls deeply asleep and awakes 20 years later to a very changed world brought about by the American Revolution which he has totally missed.

Washington Irving was an American short-story writer, essayist, biographer, historian and diplomat in the 19th century.

The Arrow and the Song

Henry Wadsworth Longfellow

I shot an arrow into the air,

It fell to earth, I knew not where;

For, so swiftly it flew, the sight

Could not follow it in its flight.

I breathed a song into the air,

It fell to earth, I knew not where;

For who has sight so keen and strong,

That it can follow the flight of song?

Long, long afterward, in an oak

I found the arrow, still unbroke;

And the song, from beginning to end,

I found again in the heart of a friend.

Answer the following questions.

1. There are _____ verses in each stanza called a couplet / tercet / quatrain.

2. The pronoun "It" in the first paragraph is referring to _____.

3. Which verse suggests that the poet did not know where the arrow had landed?

4. "For, so swiftly it flew" would be better understood if it were written "For _____
_____", which is a poetic device called
   a. personification
   b. inversion
   c. enjambment

5. Instead of "sang", the poet _____ a song, which has a more sweet-tempered / forceful connotation.

6. Why could no one find where the song had gone?

7. The word _____ is repeated twice to show how much time had passed before the arrow was found. It is an example of a poetic device called an anastrophe/epistrophe/epizeuxis.

8. Where did the poet finally find the arrow?

9. Which word suggests that the arrow was still intact?

10. Why is the word "unbroke" and not "unbroken" being used?

11. The last verse "I found again in the heart of a friend" means
    a. only part of the song was remembered
    b. the song was deeply rooted in the heart of the listener
    c. the song was sung again and again for the listener

12. In this poem, "the arrow" probably represents a toy / a wound / some harsh words, while the "song" represents a love song / a performance / an expression of kindness.

Read on:
The 'Arrow and the Song', written by Henry Wadsworth Longfellow, is a short three-stanza poem in four lines known as quatrains.

The speaker, likely to be the poet himself, is trying to depict the result of one's actions. No matter what one does in life, singing a song into the heavens or shooting an arrow into the sky, entails consequences. It could create a positive impact or a dangerously negative outcome.

Readers who enjoy this poem should also consider reading some other poems of the same poet, for example, 'A Gleam of Sunshine', 'A Psalm of Life' or 'Afternoon in February'.

Tarzan and the Golden Lion

Edgar Rice Burroughs

But today the lioness was nervous and fearful—fearful because of the single cub that remained to her—her maternal instincts centered threefold, perhaps, upon this lone and triply loved survivor—and so she did not wait for the man to threaten the safety of her little one; but instead she moved to meet him and to stop him. From the soft mother she had become a terrifying creature of destruction, her brain obsessed by a single thought—to kill.

She did not hesitate an instant at the edge of the clearing, nor did she give the slightest warning. The first intimation that the black warrior had that there was a lion within twenty miles of him, was the terrifying apparition of this devil-faced cat charging across the clearing toward him with the speed of an arrow. The black was not searching for lions. Had he known that there was one near he would have given it a wide berth. He would have fled now had there been anywhere to flee. The nearest tree was farther from him than was the lioness. She could overhaul him before he would have covered a quarter of the distance. There was no hope and there was only one thing to do. The beast was almost upon him and behind her he saw a tiny cub. The man bore a heavy spear. He carried it far back with his right hand and hurled it at the very instant that Sabor rose to seize him. The spear passed through the savage heart and almost simultaneously the giant jaws closed upon the face and skull of the warrior. The momentum of the lioness carried the two heavily to the ground, dead except for a few spasmodic twitchings of their muscles.

The orphaned cub stopped twenty feet away and surveyed the first great catastrophe of his life with questioning eyes. He wanted to approach his dam but a natural fear of the man-scent held him away. Presently he commenced to whine in a tone that always brought his mother to him hurriedly; but this time she did not come—she did not even rise and look toward him. He was puzzled—he could not understand <u>it</u>. He continued to cry, feeling all the while more sad and more lonely. Gradually he crept closer to his mother. He saw that the strange creature she had killed did not move and after a while he felt less terror of it, so that at last he found the courage to come quite close to his mother and sniff at her. He still whined to her, but she did not answer. It dawned on him at last that there was something wrong—that his great, beautiful mother was not as she had been—a change had come over her; yet still he clung to her, crying much until at last he fell asleep, cuddled close to her dead body.

It was thus that Tarzan found him—Tarzan and Jane, his wife, and their son, Korak the Killer, returning from the mysterious land of Pal-ul-don from which the two men had rescued Jane Clayton. At the sound of their approach the cub opened his eyes and rising, flattened his ears and snarled at them, backing close against his dead mother. At sight of him the <u>ape-man</u> smiled.

Answer the following questions.

1. The lioness felt _____ and _____ for she had only one cub left to her.

2. Circle the correct answer.
   The cub is described as a "lone and triply loved survivor", implying that the lioness has already lost one/two/three other cub/cubs.

3. Describe the transformation of the lioness on seeing the human as a threat to her cub.

4. Which sentence suggests that the man was totally surprised by the approach of the lioness?

5. Underline the expression (five words in the second paragraph) that means "deliberately avoided the area".

6. What might the man have done if the tree had been closer to him than the lioness?

7. It is said that "there was no hope (for the man) and there was only one thing to do". What was that only thing to do?

8. Which word in the second paragraph tells the reader that the lioness and the man were killed at the same time?

9. The first great catastrophe of the cub's life was
   a. the great fear in its heart
   b. the loss of its mother
   c. the smell of man

10. Arrange the following happenings in the correct sequence:
    _____ The lioness detected the presence of the man.
    _____ The lioness fell to the ground and died.
    _____ The lioness scratched the face and skull of the man.
    _____ The lioness was focused on killing the man.

11. If you know the story of Tarzan, you will know that the "ape-man" is referring to
    a. Tarzan
    b. Jane
    c. Korak

12. What do you think would happen to the cub?

Read on:

Tarzan, Jane Porter and Korak, on their return from adventures, have found an orphaned cub, which Tarzan adopts and takes home to heal and train. Years later, with the help of this golden lion, and a tribe of enslaved humans, Tarzan restores a queen to power, loses the diamonds given to him as a reward, and returns home with the gold he manages to attain.

Published in 1922, *Tarzan and the Golden Lion* is an adventure novel by American writer Edgar Rice Burroughs, the ninth in his series of twenty-four books about the title character Tarzan.

Peter Pan

James Matthew Barrie

In his absence things are usually quiet on the island. The fairies take an hour longer in the morning, the beasts attend to their young, the redskins feed heavily for six days and nights, and when pirates and lost boys meet they merely bite their thumbs at each other. But with the coming of Peter, who hates lethargy, they are under way again: if you put your ear to the ground now, you would hear the whole island seething with life.

On this evening the chief forces of the island were disposed as follows. The lost boys were out looking for Peter, the pirates were out looking for the lost boys, the redskins were out looking for the pirates, and the beasts were out looking for the redskins. They were going round and round the island, but they did not meet because all were going at the same rate.

All wanted blood except the boys, who liked <u>it</u> as a rule, but to-night were out to greet their captain. The boys on the island vary, of course, in numbers, according as they get killed and so on, and when they seem to be growing up, which is against the rules, Peter thins them out; but at this time there were six of them, counting the twins as two. Let us pretend to lie here among the sugar-cane and watch them as they steal by <u>in single file</u>, each with his hand on his dagger.

They are forbidden by Peter to look in the least like him, and they wear the skins of the bears slain by themselves, in which they are so round and furry that when they fall they roll. They have therefore become very sure-footed.

The first to pass is Tootles, not the least brave but the most unfortunate of all that gallant band. He had been in fewer adventures than any of them, because the big things constantly happened just when he had stepped round the corner; all would be quiet, he would take the opportunity of going off to gather a few sticks for firewood, and then when he returned the others would be sweeping up blood. This ill-luck had given a gentle melancholy to his countenance, but instead of souring his nature had sweetened to it, so that he was quite the humblest of the boys. Poor kind Tootles, there is danger in the air for you to-night. Take care lest an adventure is now offered you, which, if accepted, will plunge you in deepest woe. Tootles, the fairy Tink, who is bent on mischief this night is looking for a tool [for doing her mischief], and she thinks you are the most easily tricked of the boys. 'Ware Tinker Bell.

Would that he could hear us, but we are not really on the island, and he passes by, biting his knuckles.

Answer the following questions.

1. Give two examples to show that things are usually quiet in the absence of Peter Pan.

2. Who hates inactivity and laziness?
   a. the fairies
   b. the beasts
   c. the pirates
   d. Peter Pan

3. Underline the expression (three words in the first paragraph) which means alive with activities and movements.

4. Who were the chief forces of the island? Why didn't they meet one another?

5. What is the pronoun "it" in the first line of the third paragraph referring to?

6. What is against the rules on the island?

7. The phrase "in single file" underlined in the third paragraph means
   a. one by one
   b. line by line
   c. in a group

8. What do the boys wear? Does Peter Pan wear the same thing? Explain.

9. What is the consequence of the boy's falling and rolling in their outfits?

10. Why was Tootles the most unfortunate of all the band? What was the reason for his bad fortune?

11. Use two adjectives to describe how Tootles looked because of his bad luck.

12. The full name for the fairy "Tink" is _____.

Read on:

Peter Pan, written by J. M. Barrie, tells the story of the amazing adventures of a mischievous boy who refuses to grow up. After befriending Wendy, John and Michael in a proper middle-class home, Peter Pan flies to Neverland where he becomes the 'fairy' of a gang of lost boys and the sworn enemy of the fearsome and merciless pirate, Captain Hook, with whom Peter Pan is engaged in an ongoing war.

The main message of *Peter Pan* is that growing up is painful and leaving childhood means leaving innocence, imagination and the readiness for adventure behind.

A Daughter of the Samurai

Etsu Inagaki Sugimoto

Occasionally he would call out "A message!"—"A message!" and stop to put mail into an outstretched hand. The path was narrow and I frequently was jostled by passing people, but I was not far behind the postman when he turned into our street. I knew he would go to the side entrance with the mail; so I hurried very fast and had reached Grandmother's room and already made my bow of "I have come back," before a maid entered with the mail. The wonderful letter was for Mother, and Grandmother asked me to carry it to her.

My heart sank with disappointment; for my chance to see <u>it</u> opened was gone. I knew that, as soon as Mother received it, she would take it at once to Grandmother, but I should not be there. Then Grandmother would look at it very carefully through her big horn spectacles and hand it back to Mother, saying in a slow and ceremonious manner, "Please open!" Of course she would be agitated, because it was a foreign letter, but that would only make her still more slow and ceremonious. I could see the whole picture in my mind as I walked through the hall, carrying the big, odd-shaped envelope to Mother's room.

That evening after family service before the shrine, Grandmother kept her head bowed longer than usual. When she raised it she sat up very straight and announced solemnly, with the most formal dignity, almost like a temple service, that the young master, who had been in America for several years, was to return to his home. This was startling news, for my brother had been gone almost since I could remember and his name was never mentioned. To call him the "young master" was sufficient explanation that the unknown tragedy was past, and he reinstated in his position as a son. The servants, sitting in the rear of the room, bowed to the floor in silent congratulation, but they seemed to be struggling with suppressed excitement. I did not stop to wonder why. It was enough for me to know that my brother was coming home. I could scarcely hold the joy in my heart.

I must have been very young when my brother went away, for though I could distinctly recall the day he left, all memory of what went before or came immediately after was dim. I remember a sunny morning when our house was decorated with wondrous beauty and the servants all wore ceremonial dress with the Inagaki crest. It was the day of my brother's marriage. In the *tokonoma* of our best room was one of our treasures—a triple roll picture of pine, bamboo, and plum, painted by an ancient artist. On the platform beneath was the beautiful Takasago table where the white-haired old couple with rake and broom were gathering pine needles on the shore. Other emblems of happy married life were everywhere, for each gift—and there were whole rooms full—was decorated with small figures of snowy storks, of gold-brown tortoises, or beautiful sprays of entwined pine, bamboo, and plum.

Answer the following questions.

1. Was it easy for the writer to walk home after the postman? Explain.

2. Give two possible reasons why the writer had to bow to her grandmother.

3. What was "it" in the first line of the second paragraph referring to?

4. Did the writer's grandmother have good eyesight? How do you know?

5. True or False:
    a. The writer's grandmother would open the letter herself. _____
    b. The writer's grandmother and mother very likely did not share the same bedroom. _____

6. The writer's grandmother would feel _____ when she saw that it was a foreign letter (a letter from America in this case) most probably because _____.

7. Match the letter the family received with the correct descriptions:

	a. was big in size.
	b. was odd in shape.
The letter	c. contained startling news.
	d. brought back memories to the writer.

8. What was the significance of the brother being addressed as the "young master"?

9. Which two phrases (three words each in the third paragraph) suggest that the servants were happy to hear the news of the young master's return?

10. Though the writer remembered well the day her brother left, she could not remember
    a. it was her brother's wedding.
    b. the decorations put up.
    c. what transpired before or after her brother's departure.

11. Underline the symbols of luck for a wedding.
    Small figures/storks/gold brown colour/tortoises/table/pine/platform/bamboo/plum

12. Do you think the writer and her brother had a good relationship? Explain.

Read on:

A Daughter of the Samurai by Etsu Inagaki Sugimoto tells the true story of the youngest daughter of a high-ranking samurai and former feudal prince in the late-nineteenth-century Japan. Etsu Inagaki, originally destined to be a Buddhist priestess, is led to head an English-language mission school in Tokyo and an arranged marriage to a Japanese businessman in Cincinnati, Ohio. The momentous and the hilarious misunderstandings between the Japanese and Western ways of lives, and more importantly, the clashes of cultures, are distinctly revealed. The reader, while following the story, will be offered a glimpse of a girl's profound social changes brought about by Japanese-American relations during the Meiji period (1868–1912) as well as an insider's view of the traditional Japanese samurai family life.

A Christmas Carol

Charles Dickens

But what did Scrooge care! It was the very thing he liked. To edge his way along the crowded paths of life, warning all human sympathy to keep its distance, was what the knowing ones call 'nuts' to Scrooge.

Once upon a time—of all the good days in the year, on Christmas Eve—old Scrooge sat busy in his counting-house. It was cold, bleak, biting weather: foggy withal: and he could hear the people in the court outside, go wheezing up and down, beating their hands upon their breasts, and stamping their feet upon the pavement stones to warm them. The city clocks had only just gone three, but it was quite dark already–it had not been light all day–and candles were flaring in the windows of the neighbouring offices, like ruddy smears upon the palpable brown air. The fog came pouring in at every chink and keyhole, and was so dense without, that although the court was of the narrowest, the houses opposite were mere phantoms. To see the dingy cloud come drooping down, obscuring everything, one might have thought that Nature lived hard by, and was brewing on a large scale.

The door of Scrooge's counting-house was open that he might keep his eye upon his clerk, who in a dismal little cell beyond, a sort of tank, was copying letters. Scrooge had a very small fire, but the clerk's fire was so very much smaller that it looked like one coal. But he couldn't replenish it, for Scrooge kept the coal-box in his own room; and so surely as the clerk came in with the shovel, the master predicted that it would be necessary for them to part. Wherefore the clerk put on his white comforter, and tried to warm himself at the candle; in which effort, not being a man of a strong imagination, he failed.

'A merry Christmas, uncle! God save you!' cried a cheerful voice. It was the voice of Scrooge's nephew, who came upon him so quickly that this was the first intimation he had of his approach.

'Bah!' said Scrooge, 'Humbug!'

He had so heated himself with rapid walking in the fog and frost, this nephew of Scrooge's, that he was all in a glow; his face was ruddy and handsome; his eyes sparkled, and his breath smoked again. 'Christmas a humbug, uncle!' said Scrooge's nephew. 'You don't mean that, I am sure?'

'I do,' said Scrooge. 'Merry Christmas! What right have you to be merry? What reason have you to be merry? You're poor enough.'

'Come, then,' returned the nephew gaily. 'What right have you to be dismal? What reason have you to be morose? You're rich enough.'

Scrooge having no better answer ready on the spur of the moment, said 'Bah!' again; and followed it up with 'Humbug.'

'Don't be cross, uncle!' said the nephew.

'What else can I be,' returned the uncle, 'when I live in such a world of fools as this? Merry Christmas! Out upon merry Christmas! What's Christmas time to you but a time for paying bills without money; a time for finding yourself a year older, but not an hour richer; a time for balancing your books and having every item in 'em through a round dozen of months presented dead against you? If I could work my will,' said Scrooge indignantly, 'every idiot who goes about with "Merry Christmas" on his lips, should be boiled with his own pudding, and buried with a stake of holly through his heart. He should!'

Answer the following questions.

1. The expression which infers Scrooge had a difficult time walking along is _____ _____.

2. What adjectives are used to describe the weather of Christmas Eve that year?

3. Where was Scrooge on Christmas Eve and what do you think he was doing?

4. On this foggy night, houses were described as _____ which was an example of
   a. a simile   b. a metaphor   c. alliteration

5. Why did Scrooge keep the door of the counting-house open? Would you like to have a boss like that? Why or why not?

6. Give two examples to support the proposition that Scrooge was indeed a "scrooge."

7. What did the clerk do to try to keep himself warm?

8. "Bah!" and "Humbug!" were Scrooge's responses to his nephew's saying "_____ _____." This shows the reader that Scrooge was indeed a person who was
   a. timid and lonely   b. spoiled and deceptive   c. negative and pessimistic

9. Change the following sentence into indirect speech.
   "What reason have you to be merry? You're poor enough," Scrooge said to his nephew.
   Scrooge asked his nephew _____
   _____

10. Match Scrooge's nephew with the correct descriptions:

    | | a. was a poor but good looking boy. |
    | | b. envied his uncle's wealth. |
    | Scrooge's nephew | c. was excited about Christmas. |
    | | d. considered himself a fool. |
    | | e. was bold enough to challenge his uncle. |

11. True or False:
    a. Scrooge felt that he was smarter than most people around him. _____
    b. Scrooge started getting angrier and angrier as he talked to his nephew. _____

12. Other famous stories written by Charles Dickens are
    a. *Oliver Twist*   b. *David Copperfield*   c. *Nicholas Nickleby*   d. *The Old Curiosity Shop*

Read on

Set in London, England, in the Victorian era, the story *A Christmas Carol* opens with Ebenezer Scrooge, a mean, miserly and bitter old man, sitting in his counting-house on a freezing Christmas Eve. The story continues to recount what happens to Scrooge when he is visited by the ghost of his old business partner and then the Ghosts of Christmas Past, Present and Future. Through them, Scrooge learns the errors of his ways and wakes up on Christmas Day a different man.

Retold countless times over the years, *A Christmas Carol* retains its ability to teach the "spirit" of the season of Christmas of kindness and responsibility for those in need.

Journey to the Centre of the Earth

Jules Verne

I did not know a single word of the Danish language, and yet by a sort of mysterious instinct I understood what the guide had said.

"Water, water!" I cried, in a wild and frantic tone, clapping my hands, and gesticulating like a madman.

"Water!" murmured my uncle, in a voice of deep emotion and gratitude. "Hvar?" ("Where?")

"Nedat." ("Below.")

"Where? below!" I understood every word. I had caught the hunter by the hands, and I shook them heartily, while he looked on with perfect calmness.

The preparations for our departure did not take long, and we were soon making a rapid descent into the tunnel.

An hour later we had advanced a thousand yards, and descended two thousand feet.

At this moment I heard an accustomed and well-known sound running along the floors of the granite rock—a kind of dull and sullen roar, like that of a distant waterfall.

During the first half hour of our advance, not finding the discovered spring, my feelings of intense suffering appeared to return. Once more I began to lose all hope. My uncle, however, observing how downhearted I was again becoming, took up the conversation.

"Hans was right," he exclaimed enthusiastically; "that is the dull roaring of a torrent."

"A torrent," I cried, delighted at even hearing the <u>welcome words</u>.

"There's not the slightest doubt about it," he replied, "a subterranean river is flowing beside us."

I made no reply, but hastened on, once more animated by hope. I began not even to feel the deep fatigue which hitherto had overpowered me. The very sound of this glorious murmuring water already refreshed me. We could hear it increasing in volume every moment. The torrent, which for a long time could be heard flowing over our heads, now ran distinctly along the left wall, roaring, rushing, spluttering, and still falling.

Several times I passed my hand across the rock hoping to find some trace of humidity—of the slightest percolation. Alas! in vain.

Again a half hour passed in the same weary toil. Again we advanced.

It now became evident that the hunter, during his absence, had not been able to carry his researches any farther. Guided by an instinct peculiar to the dwellers in mountain regions and water finders, he "smelt" the living spring through the rock. Still he had not seen the precious liquid. He had neither quenched his own thirst, nor brought us one drop in his gourd.

Answer the following questions.

1. The two words, _____ and _____, are words of the French / Danish / Swedish language.

2. Was the exploring team going up or down in latitude? Explain.

3. What was the accustomed and well-known sound referring to?

4. How did the writer feel when the spring was not found?

5. What were the "welcome words" underlined in the seventh paragraph referring to?

6. True or False:
   a. The expression "animated by hope" is used to describe the excitement of the writer. _____
   b. The writer was still refreshed though the sound of the volume of the water decreased. _____

7. Which three words are used to describe the sounds made by the water? They are examples of a literary device called _____.

8. How did the writer try to find some sign of water? Was he successful? Explain.

9. Match the hunter to the following statements:

	a. was probably a man living in the mountains.
The hunter	b. was probably experienced in finding water.
	c. was able to quench his own thirst.
	d. had not returned with water.

10. Arrange the following in the correct sequence:
    _____ The writer lost hope about not finding water.
    _____ The writer still found no trace of humidity on the rock.
    _____ The words of the writer's uncle encouraged him.
    _____ The writer's team descended in the tunnel.

11. The genre of this story is
    a. fiction
    b. non-fiction
    c. autobiography

12. In your opinion, can humans arrive at the centre of the earth? Explain.

Read on:

Set in 1880, Edinburgh professor-cum-geologist Professor Otto Lidenbrock is given a piece of unusually heavy volcanic rock by his student and nephew, Axel. In the rock, Lidenbrock discovers a plumb bob bearing a cryptic inscription left by a scientist who claims he has found a passage to the centre of the earth by descending a volcano in Iceland. After translating the message, Lidenbrock and Alec set off to follow in the Icelandic pioneer's footsteps.

Another of Jules Verne's masterpieces, *Journey to the Centre of the Earth* is full of exciting action and events, and is considered a delightful book written for young people.

To Build a Fire

Jack London

He worked slowly and carefully, keenly aware of his danger. Gradually, as the flame grew stronger, he increased the size of the twigs with which he fed it. He squatted in the snow, pulling the twigs out from their entanglement in the brush and feeding directly to the flame. He knew there must be no failure. When it is seventy-five below zero, a man must not fail in his first attempt to build a fire—that is, if his feet are wet. If his feet are dry, and he fails, he can run along the trail for half a mile and restore his circulation. But the circulation of wet and freezing feet cannot be restored by running when it is seventy-five below. No matter how fast he runs, the wet feet will freeze the harder.

All this the man knew. The old-timer on Sulphur Creek had told him about it the previous fall, and now he was appreciating the advice. Already all sensation had gone out of his feet. To build the fire he had been forced to remove his mittens, and the fingers had quickly gone numb. His pace of four miles an hour had kept his heart pumping blood to the surface of his body and to all the extremities. But the instant he stopped, the action of the pump eased down. The cold of space smote the unprotected tip of the planet, and he, being on that unprotected tip, received the full force of the blow. The blood of his body recoiled before it. The blood was alive, like the dog, and like the dog it wanted to hide away and cover itself up from the fearful cold. So long as he walked four miles an hour, he pumped that blood, willy-nilly, to the surface; but now _it_ ebbed away and sank down into the recesses of his body. The extremities were the first to feel its absence. His wet feet froze the faster, and his exposed fingers numbed the faster, though they had not yet begun to freeze. Nose and cheeks were already freezing, while the skin of all his body chilled as it lost its blood.

But he was safe. Toes and nose and cheeks would be only touched by the frost, for the fire was beginning to burn with strength. He was feeding it with twigs the size of his finger. In another minute he would be able to feed it with branches the size of his wrist, and then he could remove his wet foot-gear, and, while it dried, he could keep his naked feet warm by the fire, rubbing them at first, of course, with snow. The fire was a success.

Answer the following questions.

1. The man was working slowly and carefully because he was _____ _____ .

2. Which word in the first paragraph tells us that the man was not standing?

3. What did the man put into the fire?

4. Which, dry feet or wet feet, gave the man a better chance to run? Explain.

5. From whom did the man receive advice the previous fall? Which word tells the readers that it was good advice?

6. Underline the sentence found in the second paragraph that tells the reader the man's feet had turned numb.

7. Which of the following was not what the man did to keep himself alive?
   a. He kept his pace at four miles an hour.
   b. He had to remove his mittens to build the fire.
   c. He had to stop moving to make his heart work.

8. The Tundra region is described in the second paragraph of the passage as _____ .

9. The expression "full force of the blow" is referring to
   a. the extreme coldness
   b. the punch on his face
   c. the shock of being alone

10. In what two ways was the blood in the man's body like a dog?

11. The four extremities of our body are our two _____ and _____ .

12. What gave the man hope that he would be safe?

Read on:

The man, the main character in Jack London's *To Build a Fire*, is found travelling with his dog on the Yukon Trail in the midst of an extremely cold setting of -75 degrees Fahrenheit. Together, man and dog are heading to a camp where the man will join his companions who have made an earlier start. While the dog senses the imminent danger of the utmost cold, the narrow perspective and lack of understanding of the man leads him on to eventually meet face to face nature's cruel and unforgiving indifference.

Treasure Island

Robert Louis Stevenson

I am not going to relate that voyage in detail. It was fairly prosperous. The ship proved to be a good ship, the crew were capable seamen, and the captain thoroughly understood his business. But before we came the length of Treasure Island, two or three things had happened which require to be known.

Mr. Arrow, first of all, turned out even worse than the captain had feared. He had no command among the men, and people did what they pleased with him. But that was by no means the worst of it, for after a day or two at sea he began to appear on deck with hazy eye, red cheeks, stuttering tongue, and other marks of drunkenness. Time after time he was ordered below in disgrace. Sometimes he fell and cut himself; sometimes he lay all day long in his little bunk at one side of the companion; sometimes for a day or two he would be almost sober and attend to his work at least passably.

In the meantime, we could never make out where he got drunk. That was the ship's mystery. Watch him as we pleased, we could do nothing to solve it; and when we asked him to his face, he would only laugh if he were drunk, and if he were sober deny solemnly that he ever tasted anything but water.

He was not only useless as an officer and a bad influence amongst the men, but it was plain that at this rate he must soon kill himself outright, so nobody was much surprised, nor very sorry, when one dark night, with a head sea, he disappeared entirely and was seen no more.

"Overboard!" said the captain. "Well, <u>gentlemen</u>, that saves the trouble of putting him in irons."

But there we were, without a mate; and it was necessary, of course, to <u>advance</u> one of the men. The boatswain, Job Anderson, was the likeliest man aboard, and though he kept his old title, he served in a way as mate. Mr. Trelawney had followed the sea, and his knowledge made him very useful, for he often took a watch himself in easy weather. And the coxswain, Israel Hands, was a careful, wily, old, experienced seaman who could be trusted at a pinch with almost anything.

He was a great confidant of Long John Silver, and so the mention of his name leads me on to speak of our ship's cook, Barbecue, as the men called him.

Aboard ship he carried his crutch by a lanyard round his neck, to have both hands as free as possible. It was something to see him wedge the foot of the crutch against a bulkhead, and propped against it, yielding to every movement of the ship, get on with his cooking like someone safe ashore. Still more strange was it to see him in the heaviest of weather cross the deck. He had a line or two rigged up to help him across the widest spaces–Long John's earrings, they were called; and he would hand himself from one place to another, now using the crutch, now trailing it alongside by the lanyard, as quickly as another man could walk. Yet some of the men who had sailed with him before expressed their pity to see him so reduced.

"He's no common man, Barbecue," said the coxswain to me. "He had a good schooling in his young days and can speak like a book when so minded; and brave–a lion's nothing alongside of Long John! I seen him grapple four and knock their heads together–him unarmed."

Answer the following questions.

1. What is the first announcement of the writer?

2. Match the following characters with the correct description:
   a. the captain   was the ship's cook.
   b. the crew   understood thoroughly his business.
   c. Mr. Arrow   was a drunkard.
   d. Barbecue   were capable seamen.

3. Tick against the signs of being a drunkard:
   _____ hazy eyes
   _____ red cheeks
   _____ clear speeches

4. What could Mr. Arrow do when he was a bit clear-headed?

5. What was the ship's mystery? Was it ever solved?

6. What did everybody suspect had happened when Mr. Arrow disappeared completely one dark night?

7. The underlined word "gentlemen" is referring to _____.

8. A synonym for the word "advance" in the story is
   a. move forward   b. promote   c. pay ahead of time

9. Why would the boatswain, Job Anderson, be the best candidate for being advanced to the rank of "mate"?

10. A confidant is a person one can
    a. speak to and trust fully
    b. dismiss freely
    c. order around

11. Which part of the sentence in the second last paragraph suggests Barbecue had no problems cooking on a moving ship?

12. Which of the following skills would you think makes Barbeque most valuable on the pirate ship? Explain.
    a. being able to cook   b. being literate   c. being brave

Read on:

Set in the days of sailing ships and pirates, the story follows the development of the adventures of Jim Hawkins and his search for buried treasure.

Featuring elements such as deserted tropical islands, treasure maps and pirates with parrots perched on their shoulders, the book is noted for its atmosphere, characters and action. The notion that profound satisfaction comes from the development of wisdom and self-knowledge is promoted, not so much for the search of gold.

Originally serialized in the children's magazine 'Young Folks', *Treasure Island* is an adventure novel by Scottish author Robert Louis Stevenson and has become one of the most dramatized and adapted of all novels.

The Falling Star (The War of the Worlds)

H.G. Wells

Then came the night of the first falling star. It was seen early in the morning, rushing over Winchester eastward, a line of flame high in the atmosphere. Hundreds must have seen it, and taken it for an ordinary falling star. Albin described it as leaving a greenish streak behind it that glowed for some seconds. Denning, our greatest authority on meteorites, stated that the height of its first appearance was about ninety or one hundred miles. It seemed to him that it fell to earth about one hundred miles east of him.

I was at home at that hour and writing in my study; and although my French windows face towards Ottershaw and the blind was up (for I loved in those days to look up at the night sky), I saw nothing of it. Yet this strangest of all things that ever came to earth from outer space must have fallen while I was sitting there, visible to me had I only looked up as it passed. Some of those who saw its flight say it travelled with a hissing sound. I myself heard nothing of that. Many people in Berkshire, Surrey, and Middlesex must have seen the fall of it, and, at most, have thought that another meteorite had descended. No one seems to have troubled to look for the fallen mass that night.

But very early in the morning poor Ogilvy, who had seen the shooting star and who was persuaded that a meteorite lay somewhere on the common between Horsell, Ottershaw, and Woking, rose early with the idea of finding it. Find it he did, soon after dawn, and not far from the sand pits. An enormous hole had been made by the impact of the projectile, and the sand and gravel had been flung violently in every direction over the heath, forming heaps visible a mile and a half away. The heather was on fire eastward, and a thin blue smoke rose against the dawn.

The Thing itself lay almost entirely buried in sand, amidst the scattered splinters of a fir tree it had shivered to fragments in its descent. The uncovered part had the appearance of a huge cylinder, caked over and its outline softened by a thick scaly dun-coloured incrustation. It had a diameter of about thirty yards. He approached the mass, surprised at the size and more so at the shape, since most meteorites are rounded more or less completely. It was, however, still so hot from its flight through the air as to forbid his near approach. A stirring noise within its cylinder he ascribed to the unequal cooling of its surface; for at that time it had not occurred to him that it might be hollow.

He remained standing at the edge of the pit that the Thing had made for itself, staring at its strange appearance, astonished chiefly at its unusual shape and colour, and dimly perceiving even then some evidence of design in its arrival. The early morning was wonderfully still, and the sun, just clearing the pine trees towards Weybridge, was already warm. He did not remember hearing any birds that morning, there was certainly no breeze stirring, and the only sounds were the faint movements from within the cindery cylinder. He was all alone on the common.

Answer the following questions.

1. What caused a line of flame high in the atmosphere?

2. Which three people saw the falling star?
   a. the writer
   b. Albin
   c. Denning
   d. Ogilvy

3. Give two reasons why the writer should have seen the falling star.

4. The sound the falling star made was a _____ sound which is an example of an
   a. interjection
   b. onomatopoeia
   c. exclamation

5. The sentence "No one seems to have troubled to look for the fallen mass that night." found in the second paragraph is _____ what is about to happen.
   a. announcing
   b. repeating
   c. foreshadowing

6. Did the meteorite create a deep impact? Support your answer with two pieces of evidence.

7. Could Ogilvy see the whole of the fallen object? Explain.

8. Why didn't Ogilvy go near the meteorite initially?

9. What surprised Ogilvy when he saw the object in the sand?

10. Underline the part of the sentence which suggests that Ogilvy felt the arrival of "The Thing" was not random.

11. What other names were given to falling objects in this text?

12. What would you have done if you were Ogilvy?

Read on:

The War of the Worlds, a science fiction novel by H. G. Wells, chronicles the events of a Martian invasion as experienced by the narrator and his brother.

A prominent theme in *The War of the Worlds* is that of religion: its presence and absence, the notion of a higher power, and the ability and inability to retain faith in the midst of the devastation and catastrophe of the planet earth.

The story did not appear in book form until 1898. When it was first published in the U.K., the book was well accepted by both critics and readers and has been translated into 10 languages.

The Big Four

Agatha Christie

I have met people who enjoy a channel crossing; men who can sit calmly in their deck-chairs and, on arrival, wait until the boat is moored, then gather their belongings together without fuss and disembark. Personally, I can never manage this. From the moment I get on board I feel that the time is too short to settle down to anything. I move my suit-cases from one spot to another, and if I go down to the saloon for a meal, I bolt my food with an uneasy feeling that the boat may arrive unexpectedly whilst I am below. Perhaps all this is merely a legacy from one's short leaves in the war, when it seemed a matter of such importance to secure a place near the gangway, and to be amongst the first to disembark lest one should waste precious minutes of one's three or five days' leave.

On this particular July morning, as I stood by the rail and watched the white cliffs of Dover drawing nearer, I marvelled at the passengers who could sit calmly in their chairs and never even raise their eyes for the first sight of their native land. Yet perhaps their case was different from mine. Doubtless many of them had only crossed to Paris for the week-end, whereas I had spent the last year and a half on a ranch in the Argentine. I had prospered there, and my wife and I had both enjoyed the free and easy life of the South American continent, nevertheless it was with a lump in my throat that I watched the familiar shore draw nearer and nearer.

I had landed in France two days before, transacted some necessary business, and was now *en route* for London. I should be there some months—time enough to look up old friends, and one old friend in particular. A little man with an egg-shaped head and green eyes—Hercule Poirot! I proposed to take him completely by surprise. My last letter from the Argentine had given no hint of my intended voyage—indeed, that had been decided upon hurriedly as a result of certain business complications—and I spent many amused moments picturing to myself his delight and stupefaction on beholding me.

He, I knew, was not likely to be far from his headquarters. The time when his cases had drawn him from one end of England to the other was past. His fame had spread, and no longer would he allow one case to absorb all his time. He aimed more and more, as time went on, at being considered a "consulting detective"—as much a specialist as a Harley Street physician. He had always scoffed at the popular idea of the human bloodhound who assumed wonderful disguises to track criminals, and who paused at every footprint to measure it.

"No, my friend Hastings," he would say; "we leave that to Giraud and his friends. Hercule Poirot's methods are his own. Order and method, and 'the little gray cells.' Sitting at ease in our own arm-chairs we see the things that these others overlook, and we do not jump to the conclusion like the worthy Japp."

No; there was little fear of finding Hercule Poirot far afield.

On arrival in London, I deposited my luggage at an hotel and drove straight on to the old address. What poignant memories it brought back to me! I hardly waited to greet my old landlady, but hurried up the stairs two at a time and rapped on Poirot's door.

"Enter, then," cried a familiar voice from within.

I strode in. Poirot stood facing me. In his arms he carried a small valise, which he dropped with a crash on beholding me.

"*Mon ami*, Hastings!" he cried. "*Mon ami*, Hastings!"

Answer the following questions.

1. One does a channel crossing by _____.

2. The writer
   a. could calmly sit on a deck chair.
   b. would gather his belongings without fuss before disembarking.
   c. would move his suitcase from one spot to another.
   d. would be able to enjoy his meal leisurely.

3. Which two words in the first paragraph suggest that the short leaves in the war have created certain consequence for the writer?

4. What would make the white cliffs of Dover look like they were drawing near?

5. For how many months had the writer been away in Argentina? Was he alone when he was there the whole time? Explain.

6. The expression "with a lump in my throat" suggests that the writer was feeling a bit agitated/impressed/hurt/emotional.

7. In what ways did Hercule Poirot look peculiar?

8. Why would Hercule Poirot be surprised to see the writer?

9. Poirot's "delight" and "stupefaction" in seeing the writer is an example of
   a. juxtaposition
   b. epithet
   c. polyptoton

10. What two occupations was Poirot famous for?

11. Give two pieces of evidence that show Poirot saw himself superior to other detectives.

12. What is the author, Agatha Christie, most famous for?

Read on:

The Big Four, written by Agatha Christie and first published in 1927, is a novel featuring Hercule Poirot, Arthur Hastings and Inspector Japp. This is a tale of international intrigue and espionage, with Poirot seeking help from both old and new friends when facing a dangerous group of dissidents responsible for a series of violent murders.

Hope

Emily Elizabeth Dickinson

Hope is the thing with feathers

That perches in the soul,

And sings the tune without the words,

And never stops at all,

And sweetest in the gale is heard;

And sore must be the storm

That could abash the little bird

That kept so many warm.

I've heard it in the chillest land,

And on the strangest sea;

Yes, never, in extremity,

It asked a crumb of me.

Hope

Max Ehrmann

Deny me all the good of earth —

All joy and soul-rebounding mirth,

All wealth and rank and love's great days;

But leave one thing by which to cope

With ebbing life's dim evening rays —

Leave me but hope.

Answer the following questions.

1. What is hope compared to that perches in the soul?

2. "Hope is the thing with feathers" is an example of
   a. a simile
   b. a metaphor
   c. personification

3. Which line tells us that the tune without words goes on and on?

4. The conjunction "And" is used at the beginning of four lines. It is an example of
   a. an epizeuxis
   b. asyndeton
   c. polysyndeton

5. What could the storm do to the little bird?

6. The pronoun "it" in the first line of the last stanza of the first poem is referring to _____.

7. Which two verses tell us that hope is everywhere in this world?

8. Does hope ever ask for anything in return? Quote two lines to support your answer.

9. The poet writes this poem
   a. to arouse sympathy
   b. to lift up spirits
   c. to describe life

10. In 'Hope' by Max Ehrmann, the word 'All' is repeated at the beginning of the second and third verses of the poem. The poetic device employed is called an anaphora / epistrophe.

11. According to Ehrmann, hope is most needed to cope with _____.

12. The mood and tone of the poem 'Hope' by Max Ehrmann is
    a. optimistic
    b. pessimistic
    c. bitter

Read on:

In the poem 'Hope', written by American poet Emily Dickenson, the image of a bird, a thing of feathers, is metaphorically used to describe the qualities of hope. It lives in the soul of a human, and it sings no matter what. Hope, in short, helps us to weather storms and overcome hardships. 'Hope' by Max Erhmann is found in his fifth book *The Desiderata of Hope* that comprises poems on the theme of hope to inspire courage in the face of adversity and the most trying of times.

The Great Gatsby

F. Scott Fitzgerald

There was music from my neighbor's house through the summer nights. In his blue gardens men and girls came and went like moths among the whisperings and the champagne and the stars. At high tide in the afternoon, I watched his guests diving from the tower of his raft or taking the sun on the hot sand of his beach while his two motor boats slit the waters of the Sound, drawing aquaplanes over cataracts of foam. On week-ends his Rolls-Royce became an omnibus, bearing parties to and from the city, between nine in the morning and long past midnight, while his station wagon scampered like a brisk yellow bug to meet all the trains. And on Mondays eight servants including an extra gardener toiled all day with mops and scrubbing-brushes and hammers and garden shears, repairing the ravages of the night before.

Every Friday five crates of oranges and lemons arrived from a fruiterer in New York – every Monday these same oranges and lemons left his back door in a pyramid of pulpless halves. There was a machine in the kitchen which could extract the juice of two hundred oranges in half an hour, if a little button was pressed two hundred times by a butler's thumb.

At least once a fortnight a corps of caterers came down with several hundred feet of canvas and enough colored lights to make a Christmas tree of Gatsby's enormous garden. On buffet tables, garnished with glistening hors d'oeuvre, spiced baked hams crowded against salads of harlequin designs and pastry pigs and turkeys bewitched to a dark gold. In the main hall a bar with a real brass rail was set up, and stocked with gins and liquors and with cordials so long forgotten that most of his female guests were too young to know one from the other.

By seven o'clock the orchestra has arrived – no thin five piece affair but a whole pit full of oboes and trombones and saxophones and viols and cornets and piccolos and low and high drums. The last swimmers have come in from the beach now and are dressing upstairs; the cars from New York are parked five deep in the drive, and already the halls and salons and verandas are gaudy with primary colors and hair shorn in strange new ways and shawls beyond the dreams of Castile. The bar is in full swing and floating rounds of cocktails permeate the garden outside until the air is alive with chatter and laughter and casual innuendo and introductions forgotten on the spot and enthusiastic meetings between women who never knew each other's names.

The lights grow brighter as the earth lurches away from the sun, and now the orchestra is playing yellow cocktail music, and the opera of voices pitches a key higher. Laughter is easier minute by minute, spilled with prodigality, tipped out at a cheerful word.

Answer the following questions.

1. Through the summer nights, _____ could be heard from the writer's neighbour's house.

2. What were the visitors who came to the parties compared to?

3. One activity that the guests would not be engaged in during the afternoon was
   a. diving
   b. sunbathing
   c. motor-boating
   d. dancing

4. Were the two vehicles, a Rolls-Royce and a station wagon, well used on weekends? Explain.

5. What tools were needed on Mondays to repair the extensive damage caused? Who caused the damage?

6. What would happen on Monday to the crates of oranges and lemons that arrived from New York? What would they have been used for making?

7. Was the juice hand-pressed? Explain.

8. What would the Christmas tree in Gatsby's enormous garden be made of?

9. Would most of the female guests know all the liquors they were drinking? Why or why not?

10. Underline two expressions that tell us that it was a full orchestra with all kinds of instruments employed.

11. Arrange the following sentences in the correct sequence:
    _____ The orchestra arrived with all sorts of musical instruments.
    _____ Cocktails were being served to all guests who had arrived.
    _____ Servants mopped and scrubbed and hammered and sheared to repair all damage done.
    _____ Guests enjoyed themselves diving or basking in the sun.

12. The detailed descriptions of Gatsby's parties suggest that Gatsby was a person who was very
    a. mysterious
    b. pompous
    c. domineering

Read on:

Authored by American writer F. Scott Fitzgerald, *The Great Gatsby* is a tragic love story set on Long Island near New York City in the Jazz Age. Nick Carraway's interactions with millionaire Jay Gatsby and Gatsby's obsession to be reunited with his former lover, Daisy Buchanan, are brilliantly detailed.

Though a commercial disappointment when it was first published, this novel became a core part of most American high school curricula and a part of American popular culture.

The Painted Veil

W. Somerset Maugham

Vaguely she knew that terrible things were happening there, not from Walter who when she questioned him (for otherwise he rarely spoke to her) answered with a humorous nonchalance which sent a shiver down her spine; but from Waddington and from the amah. The people were dying at the rate of a hundred a day, and hardly any of those who were attacked by the disease recovered from it; the gods had been brought out from the abandoned temples and placed in the streets; offerings were laid before them and sacrifices made, but they did not stay the plague. The people died so fast that it was hardly possible to bury them. In some houses the whole family had been swept away and there was none to perform the funeral rights. The officer commanding the troops was a masterful man and if the city was not given over to riot and arson it was due to his determination. He forced his soldiers to bury such as there was no one else to bury and he had shot with his own hand an officer who demurred at entering a stricken house.

Kitty sometimes was so frightened that her heart sank within her and she would tremble in every limb. It was very well to say that the risk was small if you took reasonable precautions: she was panic-stricken. She turned over in her mind crazy plans of escape. To get away, just to get away, she was prepared to set out as she was and make her way alone, without anything but what she stood up in, to some place of safety. She thought of throwing herself on the mercy of Waddington, telling him everything and beseeching him to help her to get back to Tching-Yen. If she flung herself on her knees before her husband, and admitted that she was frightened, frightened, even though he hated her now he must have enough human feeling in him to pity her.

It was out of the question. If she went, where could she go? Not to her mother; her mother would make her see very plainly that, having married her off, she counted on being rid of her; and besides she did not want to go to her mother. She wanted to go to Charlie, and he did not want her. She knew what he would say if she suddenly appeared before him. She saw the sullen look of his face and the shrewd hardness behind his charming eyes. It would be difficult for him to find words that sounded well. She clenched her hands. She would have given anything to humiliate him as he had humiliated her.

Answer the following questions.

1. The writer knew a little that terrible things were happening there from _____ and _____ and not from _____.

2. The disease was described to be very serious because
   a. people were dying at a thousand a day.
   b. not many who were attacked by it recovered from it.
   c. people died so fast that it was scarcely possible to bury them.
   d. in some houses, everyone died.

3. Was the community a religious one? How do you know?

4. If the commanding officer had not been determined, _____ and _____ would have occurred.

5. Why did the commanding officer shoot an officer with his own hand?

6. Underline the expression (six words in the second paragraph) which means "it sounded good and satisfactory".

7. True or False:
   a. Kitty had made a firm decision to escape. _____
   b. Kitty was very calm when she tried to work out plans of escape. _____

8. Kitty thought of asking her husband to help though she knew he _____ her because he might _____ her.

9. Match the following characters with the correct description:
   Waddington   wanted to get rid of Kitty.
   Walter (Kitty's husband)   might be able to help Kitty go home.
   Kitty's mother   might help if Kitty knelt before him.
   Charlie   had humiliated Kitty.

10. The description of Charlie, "the shrewd hardness behind his charming eyes", is an example of
    a. comparison
    b. juxtaposition
    c. hyperbole

11. Why didn't Kitty want to talk to Charlie again?

12. The tone of this passage is
    a. comical
    b. sarcastic
    c. serious

Read on:

First published in 1925, *The Painted Veil* is set in England and Hong Kong in the 1920s. A beautiful but materialistic and vain Kitty Garstin is forced to accompany her husband to a remote village in China ravaged by a cholera outbreak.

In the story, Somerset Maugham uses third-person-limited point of view (through the eyes of Kitty) to dig deeply into a society of people whose lives are tainted, as if seem through a painted veil.

Les Misérables

Victor Hugo

Jean Valjean saw the obstacle. At all hazards the opening must be made still wider.

He so determined, and pushed the door a third time, harder than before. This time a rusty hinge suddenly sent out into darkness a harsh and prolonged creak.

Jean Valjean shivered. The noise of this hinge sounded in his ears as clear and terrible as the trumpet of Judgment Day.

In the fantastic exaggeration of the first moment, he almost imagined that this hinge had become animate, and suddenly endowed with a terrible life; and that it was barking like a dog to warn everybody, and rouse the sleepers.

He stopped, shuddering and distracted, and dropped from his tiptoes to his feet. He felt the pulses of his temples beat like trip-hammers, and it appeared to him that his breath came from his chest with the roar of wind from a cavern. It seemed impossible that the horrible sound of this incensed hinge had not shaken the whole house with a shock of an earthquake; the door pushed by him had taken alarm, and had called out; the old man would arise, the two old women would scream; help would come; in a quarter of an hour the town would be alive with it, and the gendarmes in pursuit. For a moment he thought he was lost.

He stood still, petrified like a pillar of salt, not daring to stir. Some minutes passed. The door was wide open; he ventured a look into the room. Nothing had moved. He listened. Nothing was stirring in the house. The noise of the rusty hinge had wakened nobody.

This first danger was over, but still he felt within him a frightful tumult. Nevertheless, he did not flinch. Not even when he thought he was lost had he flinched. His only thought was to make an end of it quickly. He took one step and was inside.

A deep calm filled the chamber. Here and there indistinct, dim forms could be distinguished; which by day, were papers scattered over a table, open folios, books piled on a stool, an arm-chair with clothes on it, a prayer stool, but now were only dark corners and whitish spots. Jean Valjean advanced, carefully avoiding the furniture. At the further end of the room he could hear the regular, quiet breathing of the sleeping bishop.

Suddenly he stopped: he was near the bed, he had reached it sooner than he thought.

Nature sometimes joins her effects and her appearances to our acts with a sort of gloomy, intelligent appropriateness, as if <u>she</u> would compel us to reflect. For nearly a half hour a great cloud had darkened the sky. At the moment when Jean Valjean paused before the bed the cloud broke as if purposely, and a ray of moonlight crossing the high window, suddenly lighted up the bishop's pale face. He slept tranquilly. He was almost entirely dressed, though in bed, on account of the cold nights of the lower Alps, with a dark woollen garment which covered his arms to the wrists. His head had fallen on the pillow in the unstudied attitude of slumber; over the side of the bed hung his hand, ornamented with the pastoral ring, and <u>which</u> had done so many good deeds, so many pious acts. His entire countenance was lit up with a vague expression of content, hope, and happiness. It was more than a smile and almost a radiance. On his forehead rested the indescribable reflection of an unseen light. The souls of the upright in sleep have vision of a mysterious heaven.

Answer the following questions.

1. True or False:
   a. Jean Valjean could not see what was barring the entrance to the room. _____
   b. Jean Valjean was determined to go into the room. _____

2. When the door was pushed the third time,
   a. it yielded gradually and silently.
   b. it sent a soft and prolonged creak.
   c. it made Jean Valjean shiver.

3. Underline the correct answers.
   "The noise of this hinge sounded in his ears as clear and terrible as the trumpet of the Judgment Day" is an example of a simile/metaphor/personification and an example of a literary technique called illusion/allusion/hallucination.

4. Underline the part of the sentence between the third and sixth paragraphs that suggests that Jean Valjean had tried not to make any noise on approaching the door.

5. Jean Valjean was anticipating the consequences of the noise to happen in the following sequence:
   _____ The military officers would come.
   _____ The whole town would come alive.
   _____ The old man would get up.
   _____ The old women would scream.

6. Would Valjean feel a sense of relief when he looked into the room? Explain.

7. The writer mentioned the fact that Jean Valjean did not flinch twice. It was to
   a. emphasise that Jean Valjean was petrified.
   b. emphasise that Jean Valjean was distracted.
   c. emphasise that Jean Valjean stayed calm despite his fear.

8. What made Valjean stop advancing all of a sudden?

9. Why were all the items in the room appearing in indistinct dim forms?

10. What are the pronouns "she" and "which" underlined in the last paragraph referring to?

11. In what way was nature helping?

12. Underline the sentence in the last paragraph which means "good people sleep peacefully and see heaven in their slumber".

Read on:

Les Misérables, an epic story of heroism, desperation and redemption, has spawned plays, movies, countless adaptations and abridgements.

Les Misérables follows the dramatically unfortunate life of Jean Valjean, who is sentenced to five years of hard labour for having stolen a loaf of bread to feed his hungry sister and her seven children. On being discharged after 19 years, because of his repeated but failed attempts to escape, Valjean's encounter with a God-fearing bishop allows him to start anew, yet the police inspector is bent on capturing and convicting the protagonist again.

The Time Machine

Chapter 12
H. G. Wells

'So I came back. For a long time I must have been insensible upon the machine. The blinking succession of the days and nights was resumed, the sun got golden again, the sky blue. I breathed with greater freedom. The fluctuating contours of the land <u>ebbed and flowed</u>. The hands spun backward upon the dials. At last I saw again the dim shadows of houses, the evidences of decadent humanity. These, too, changed and passed, and others came. Presently, when the million dial was at zero, I slackened speed. I began to recognize our own petty and familiar architecture, the thousands hand ran back to the starting-point, the night and day flapped slower and slower. Then the old walls of the laboratory came round me. Very gently, now, I slowed the mechanism down.

'I saw one little thing that seemed odd to me. I think I have told you that when I set out, before my velocity became very high, Mrs. Watchett had walked across the room, travelling, as it seemed to me, like a rocket. As I returned, I passed again across that minute when she traversed the laboratory. But now her every motion appeared to be the exact inversion of her previous ones. The door at the lower end opened, and she glided quietly up the laboratory, back foremost, and disappeared behind the door by which she had previously entered. Just before that I seemed to see Hillyer for a moment; but he passed like a flash.

'Then I stopped the machine, and saw about me again the old familiar laboratory, my tools, my appliances just as I had left them. I got off the thing very shakily, and sat down upon my bench. For several minutes I trembled violently. Then I became calmer. Around me was my old workshop again, exactly as it had been. I might have slept there, and the whole thing have been a dream.

'And yet, not exactly! The thing had started from the south-east corner of the laboratory. It had come to rest again in the north-west, against the wall where you saw it. That gives you the exact distance from my little lawn to the pedestal of the White Sphinx, into which the Morlocks had carried my machine.

'For a time my brain went stagnant. Presently I got up and came through the passage here, limping, because my heel was still painful, and feeling sorely begrimed. I saw the PALL MALL GAZETTE on the table by the door. I found the date was indeed to-day, and looking at the timepiece, saw the hour was almost eight o'clock. I heard your voices and the clatter of plates. I hesitated—I felt so sick and weak. Then I sniffed good wholesome meat, and opened the door on you. You know the rest. I washed, and dined, and now I am telling you the story.

'I know,' he said, after a pause, 'that all this will be absolutely incredible to you. To me the one incredible thing is that I am here to-night in this old familiar room looking into your friendly faces and telling you these strange adventures.'

Answer the following questions.

1. The first sentence "So I came back." suggests that the writer had been _____ else.

2. Which word in the first paragraph indicates that the writer had been unconscious in the machine?

3. The expression "ebbed and flowed" is usually used to describe
   a. the sea
   b. the land
   c. the clouds

4. Underline the phrase (three words in the first paragraph) that indicates that the writer was feeling fairly negative about the human race.

5. According to the first paragraph, was time going faster or slower? Give evidence.

6. Did the writer see Hillyer for a long time? How do you know?

7. True or False:
   a. Everything in the laboratory looked the same to the writer upon his return. _____
   b. The writer felt that the whole experience he had had seemed unreal. _____

8. What convinced the writer that he had not been dreaming?

9. Match the machine with the correct descriptions:

	a. had hands and dials to control the time.
	b. was a rocket.
The machine	c. had come to rest against a wall.
	d. had been carried by the Morlocks.
	e. had allowed the writer to daydream.

10. The writer could not _____ well because his brain had gone stagnant and he could not _____ because his heel was still painful.

11. The *Pall Mall Gazette* was probably the town's
    a. newspaper
    b. directory
    c. business review

12. The story "The Time Machine" is an example of realistic fiction/science fiction/historical fiction as it deals with time travel.

Read on:

The Time Machine, a science fiction novel published in 1895 by H. G. Wells, has indirectly inspired many later works of fiction that feature journeying through the dimension of time.

When the Time Traveller steps out of his machine for the first time, he finds himself in the year 802,700. There he discovers two bizarre races who do not only exhibit the duality of human nature, but also the symbolic yet terrifying portrait of the future of man.

The term "time machine", coined by H. G. Wells, is used to refer to a vehicle that can travel purposely forward and backward through time.

Twenty Thousand Leagues Under the Sea

Jules Verne

"Do not excite yourself, Ned," I said to the harpooner, "and do not compromise us by useless "violence. Who knows that they will not listen to us? Let us rather try to find out where we are."

I groped about. In five steps I came to an iron wall, made of plates bolted together. Then turning back I struck against a wooden table, near which were ranged several stools. The boards of this prison were concealed under a thick mat, which deadened the noise of the feet. The bare walls revealed no trace of window or door. Conseil, going round the reverse way, met me, and we went back to the middle of the cabin, which measured about twenty feet by ten. As to its height, Ned Land, in spite of his own great height, could not measure it.

Half an hour had already passed without our situation being bettered, when the dense darkness suddenly gave way to extreme light. Our prison was suddenly lighted, that is to say, it became filled with a luminous matter, so strong that I could not bear it at first. In its whiteness and intensity I recognised that electric light which played round the submarine boat like a magnificent phenomenon of phosphorescence. After shutting my eyes involuntarily, I opened them, and saw that this luminous agent came from a half globe, unpolished, placed in the roof of the cabin.

"At last one can see," cried Ned Land, who, knife in hand, stood on the defensive.

"Yes," said I; "but we are still in the dark about ourselves."

"Let master have patience," said the imperturbable Conseil.

The sudden lighting of the cabin enabled me to examine it minutely. It only contained a table and five stools. The invisible door might be hermetically sealed. No noise was heard. All seemed dead in the interior of this boat. Did it move, did it float on the surface of the ocean, or did it dive into its depths? I could not guess.

A noise of bolts was now heard, the door opened, and two men appeared.

One was short, very muscular, broad-shouldered, with robust limbs, strong head, an abundance of black hair, thick moustache, a quick penetrating look, and the vivacity which characterises the population of Southern France.

The second stranger merits a more detailed description. I made out his prevailing qualities directly: self-confidence—because his head was well set on his shoulders, and his black eyes looked around with cold assurance; calmness—for his skin, rather pale, showed his coolness of blood; energy—evinced by the rapid contraction of his lofty brows; and courage—because his deep breathing denoted great power of lungs.

Answer the following questions.

1. The writer advised the harpooner who was in a/an _____ state of mind not to use violence as they might be _____ too.

2. The sentence "I groped about" suggests that
   a. the writer could not think at all.
   b. the writer was wandering about.
   c. the writer could not see well.

3. What helped to reduce the noise made by the feet?

4. Could anyone see anything on the outside of the cabin? Why or why not?

5. Was Ned Land a tall man? Underline the part of the sentence that suggests that.

6. Which two words in the third paragraph are used in contrast to "extreme light"?

7. What caused the prison to become extremely bright all of a sudden?

8. How does the reader know that Ned Land was ready to defend himself?

9. Underline the part of the sentence which suggests that the team of people still did not know what their current situation was.

10. Change the following adjectives to the opposite by supplying the correct prefixes only once (in; un; im; dis).
    a. _____perturbable
    b. _____considerate
    c. _____professional
    d. _____connected

11. Could the writer answer any of his own queries? Which line tells us that?

12. Match the two strangers with the correct descriptions:

	a. looked confident and calm.
The first stranger	b. had more prominent physical attributes.
	c. looked energetic and courageous.
The second stranger	d. was probably a Frenchman.
	e. deserves a more detailed description.

Read on:

Twenty Thousand Leagues Under the Sea is a hard science fiction written by French writer Jules Verne, originally published in 1870.

The story, told through the eyes of marine biologist, Pierre Aronnax, recounts how he is thrown into the sea together with two companions, after the hunt of a gigantic mysterious "sea monster" which turns out to be a technologically advanced submarine belonging to Captain Nemo.

After sequence episodes of amazing, unexpected events and situations of danger, the three-man team finally escapes to return to land. The overall story is riveting and full of dramatic revelations, and remains a renowned classic science fiction adventure novel.

The Open Window

Saki

"You may wonder why we keep that window wide open on an October afternoon," said the niece, indicating a large French window that opened on to a lawn.

"It is quite warm for the time of the year," said Framton; "but has that window got anything to do with the tragedy?"

"Out through that window, three years ago to a day, her husband and her two young brothers went off for their day's shooting. They never came back. In crossing the moor to their favourite snipe-shooting ground they were all three engulfed in a treacherous piece of bog. It had been that dreadful wet summer, you know, and places that were safe in other years gave way suddenly without warning. Their bodies were never recovered. That was the dreadful part of it." Here the child's voice lost its self-possessed note and became falteringly human. "Poor aunt always thinks that they will come back someday, they and the little brown spaniel that was lost with them, and walk in at that window just as they used to do. That is why the window is kept open every evening till it is quite <u>dusk</u>. Poor dear aunt, she has often told me how they went out, her husband with his white waterproof coat over his arm, and Ronnie, her youngest brother, singing 'Bertie, why do you bound?' as he always did to tease her, because she said it got on her nerves. Do you know, sometimes on still, quiet evenings like this, I almost get a creepy feeling that they will all walk in through that window -"

She broke off with a little shudder. It was a relief to Framton when the aunt bustled into the room with a whirl of apologies for being late in making her appearance.

"I hope Vera has been amusing you?" she said.

"She has been very interesting," said Framton.

"I hope you don't mind the open window," said Mrs. Sappleton briskly; "my husband and brothers will be home directly from shooting, and they always come in this way. They've been out for snipe in the marshes today, so they'll make a fine mess over my poor carpets. So like you menfolk, isn't it?"

She rattled on cheerfully about the shooting and the scarcity of birds, and the prospects for duck in the winter. To Framton it was all purely horrible. He made a <u>desperate</u> but only <u>partially</u> successful effort to turn the talk on to a less ghastly topic, he was <u>conscious</u> that his hostess was giving him only a fragment of her attention, and her eyes were constantly straying past him to the open window and the lawn beyond. It was certainly an unfortunate coincidence that he should have paid his visit on this <u>tragic</u> anniversary.

"The doctors agree in ordering me complete rest, an absence of mental excitement, and avoidance of anything in the nature of violent physical exercise," announced Framton, who laboured under the tolerably widespread delusion that total strangers and chance acquaintances are hungry for the least detail of one's ailments and infirmities, their cause and cure. "On the matter of diet they are not so much in agreement," he continued.

"No?" said Mrs. Sappleton, in a voice which only replaced a yawn at the last moment. Then she suddenly brightened into alert attention - but not to what Framton was saying.

"Here they are at last!" she cried. "Just in time for tea, and don't they look as if they were muddy up to the eyes!"

Framton shivered slightly and turned towards the niece with a look intended to convey sympathetic comprehension. The child was staring out through the open window with a dazed horror in her eyes. In a chill shock of nameless fear Framton swung round in his seat and looked in the same direction.

Answer the following questions.

1. Framton could see the lawn through a large _____.

2. Framton was led to believe _____ had happened before he arrived.
   a. something very sad
   b. something very exciting
   c. something very interesting

3. Who and what were in the hunting party?

4. What had happened to the hunting party according to the young niece?

5. Underline the sentence in the third paragraph that tells the reader that the young niece suddenly lost her confidence and seemed to be fearful herself.

6. "Dusk" is the time
   a. between darkness and sunrise.
   b. between morning and noon.
   c. between sunset and darkness.
   d. between sunset and midnight.

7. Circle the correct answer.
   When something gets on your nerves, you feel comforted/irritated/amused/frightened.

8. How did Framton feel when Mrs. Sappleton made her appearance? Explain.

9. Why would the hunting party make a fine mess over the carpets?

10. Provide the abstract nouns for the following words:
    E.g. scarce - <u>scarcity</u>
    a. desperate - _____
    b. partial - _____
    c. conscious - _____
    d. tragic - _____

11. Was Mrs. Sappleton interested in the medical condition of Framton? How do you know?

12. When Framton "turned towards the niece with a look intended to convey sympathetic comprehension",
    a. he meant to show understanding of what the niece had said before about her aunt's delusion.
    b. he wanted to get sympathy from the niece.
    c. he wanted to check on the mental status of the niece.

Read on:

One of Saki's most successful and best-known stories, 'The Open Window' follows the account of a spontaneous practical joke played upon a visiting stranger, Mr. Nuttel, a man in need of a cure for his nerves, by a mischievous but quick-witted young girl, niece of the waited on matron of the house.

Search for Mr. Hyde

Robert Louis Stevenson

Mr. Utterson sighed deeply but said never a word; and the young man presently resumed. "Here is another lesson to say nothing," said he. "I am ashamed of my long tongue. Let us make a bargain never to refer to this again."

"With all my heart," said the lawyer. "I shake hands on that, Richard."

That evening Mr. Utterson came home to his bachelor house in sombre spirits and sat down to dinner without relish. It was his custom of a Sunday, when this meal was over, to sit close by the fire, a volume of some dry divinity on his reading desk, until the clock of the neighbouring church rang out the house of twelve, when he would go soberly and gratefully to bed. On this night however, as soon as the cloth was taken away, he took up a candle and went into his business room. There he opened his safe, took from the most private part of it a document endorsed on the envelope as Dr. Jekyll's Will and sat down with a clouded brow to study its contents. The will was holograph, for Mr. Utterson though he took charge of it now that it was made, had refused to lend the least assistance in the making of it; it provided not only that, in case of the decease of Henry Jekyll, M.D., D.C.L., L.L.D., F.R.S., etc., all his possessions were to pass into the hands of his "friend and benefactor Edward Hyde," but that in case of Dr. Jekyll's "disappearance of unexplained absence for any period exceeding three calendar months," the said Edward Hyde should step into the said Henry Jekyll's shoes without further delay and free from any burthen or obligation beyond the payment of a few small sums to the members of the doctor's household. This document had long been the lawyer's eyesore. It offended him both as a lawyer and as a lover of the sane and customary sides of life, to whom the fanciful was the immodest. And hitherto it was his ignorance of Mr. Hyde that had swelled his indignation; now, by a sudden turn, it was his knowledge. It was already bad enough when the name was but a name of which he could learn no more. It was worse when it began to be clothed upon with the detestable attributes; and out of the shifting, insubstantial mists that had so long baffled his eye, there leaped up the sudden, definite presentment of a fiend.

"I thought it was madness," he said, as he replaced the obnoxious paper in the safe, "and now I begin to fear it is disgrace."

With that he blew out his candle, put on a greatcoat, and set forth in the direction of Cavendish Square, that citadel of medicine, where his friend, the great Dr. Lanyon, had his house and received his crowding patients. "If anyone knows, it will be Lanyon," he had thought. The solemn butler knew and welcomed him; he was subjected to no stage of delay, but ushered direct from the door to the dining-room where Dr. Lanyon sat alone over his wine. This was a hearty, healthy, dapper, red-faced gentleman, with a shock of hair prematurely white, and a boisterous and decided manner. At sight of Mr. Utterson, he sprang up from his chair and welcomed him with both hands. The geniality, as was the way of the man, was somewhat theatrical to the eye; but it reposed on genuine feeling. For these two were old friends, old mates both at school and college, both thorough respectors of themselves and of each other, and what does not always follow, men who thoroughly enjoyed each other's company.

Answer the following questions.

1. The reader knows that Mr. Utterson was married/unmarried because he lived in a _____.

2. Which was not Mr. Utterson's custom of a Sunday?
   a. sitting near to the fire after his meal
   b. working in his business room before retiring to bed
   c. going to bed at twelve

3. Mr. Utterson took from it a document endorsed on the envelope as Dr. Jekyll's Will. What is "it" referring to?

4. True or False:
   a. Henry Jekyll was leaving all his money to Mr. Hyde. _____
   b. Henry Jekyll considered Mr. Hyde his friend and benefactor. _____

5. What and to whom did Mr. Hyde have to pay for getting all that Henry Jekyll left to him?

6. Did Mr. Utterson like the way the will was made? Use three pieces of evidence in the third paragraph to support your answer?

7. The will's being referred to as an "obnoxious paper" is an example of a literary technique called
   a. a simile
   b. alliteration
   c. metonymy

8. In what way do you think Mr. Utterson thought Dr. Lanyon might be able to help him out?

9. Was Dr. Lanyon a man of affluence himself? What makes you think that?

10. Did Dr. Lanyon look younger or older than his real age? Find evidence in the last paragraph to support your answer.

11. The way this passage is written foreshadows
    a. a day of preparation for a will
    b. the coming of a series of mysterious events
    c. an emotional ending

12. In modern language, what kind of a person is a Jekyll and Hyde?

Read on:

The family lawyer of Dr. Jekyll, after reading the will of his friend, starts being worried and concerned over the instructions set in the will that in the event of Dr. Jekyll's disappearance, all his possessions, but little to be left to the domestic staff, will go to a Mr. Hyde. Utterson thus decides to call on Dr. Lanyon, an old friend of his and Jekyll's, for some light to be shed on the situation.

Answers

Daddy-Long-Legs

1. Madison Avenue; big; forbidding
2. to get up her courage
3. a. looked like a fatherly old man.
   b. made Judy feel at home at once.
   d. cared for Mr. Smith a lot.
4. b. solemn
5. the butler
6. "my feet would hardly take me up"
7. Mr. Smith had been very ill and it was the first day he had been allowed to sit up
8. b. could not see anything clearly.
9. to make him feel warmer and more comfortable
10. c. dramatic pauses
11. disrespectful
12. "In an instant it flashed over me."

Rip Van Winkle

1. wild; lonely; shagged
2. c. personification
3. to face the fierce looks and harsh scoldings of his wife
4. "solitary"
5. "He thought his fancy must have deceived him,"
6. dog; bristled up his back / a low growl / skulked to his master's side
7. anxious
8. a. heavy
9. He hastened to give assistance to the stranger.
10. a. True
    b. False
    c. False
11. No—Rip and his companion had laboured on in silence
12. 2 1 4 3

The Arrow and the Song

1. four; quatrain
2. the arrow
3. "It fell to earth, I knew not where;"
4. it flew so swiftly; b. inversion
5. breathed; sweet-tempered
6. no one had sight so keen and strong to follow it
7. long ; epizeuxis
8. in an oak
9. "unbroke"
10. to rhyme with 'oak'
11. b. the song was deeply rooted in the heart of the listener
12. some harsh words; an expression of kindness

Tarzan and the Golden Lion

1. nervous; fearful
2. two; cubs
3. She changed from a soft mother to a terrifying creature of destruction.
4. The first intimation that the black warrior had that there was a lion within twenty miles of him, was the terrifying apparition of this devil-faced cat charging across the clearing toward him with the speed of an arrow.
5. "given it a wide berth"
6. He might have tried to climb up the tree.
7. to hurl the heavy spear at the lioness
8. "simultaneously"
9. b. the loss of its mother
10. 1 4 3 2
11. a. Tarzan
12. It would be adopted by Tarzan (Tarzan's family).

Peter Pan

1. the fairies take an hour longer in the morning; the beasts attend to the young; the redskins feed heavily for six days and nights; pirates and lost boys merely bite their thumbs at each other when they meet (any two answers accepted)
2. Peter Pan
3. seething with life
4. The lost boys, the pirates, the redskins and the beasts; all were going at the same rate
5. "blood"
6. to grow up
7. a. one by one
8. skins of bears slained by themselves;
   No—no one could look in the least like him

9. they have become very sure-footed
10. he had been in fewer adventures than any others; the big things constantly happened just when he had stepped around the corner
11. gentle, melancholy, humble (any two answers accepted)
12. Tinker Bell

A Daughter of the Samurai

1. No—the path was narrow and she was frequently jostled by other people
2. 1. to announce she had returned to the house
    2. to show her respect
3. the mail
4. No—she was wearing big horn spectacles
5. a. False
    b. True
6. agitated; she could not read English
7. a. was big in size.
    b. was odd in shape.
    c. contained startling news.
    d. brought back memories to the writer.
8. the unknown tragedy was past and the brother was reinstated in his position as a son.
9. "in silent congratulation"; "with suppressed excitement"
10. c. what transpired before or after her brother's departure.
11. storks; golden brown colour; tortoises; pine; bamboo; plum
12. Yes—the girl could scarcely hold the joy in her heart
    No—they never wrote to each other after the brother had gone to America

A Christmas Carol

1. "to edge his way"
2. cold, bleak, biting and foggy
3. in his counting-house, counting his money
4. phantoms; b. a metaphor
5. to keep his eye upon his clerk
    No—no one would like to be watched while working
6. Scrooge had a small fire; the clerk's fire was so very much smaller that it looked like one coal; Scrooge kept the coal-box in his own room so that the clerk couldn't replenish it (any two answers accepted)
7. He put on his white comforter and tried to warm himself at the candle.
8. A merry Christmas, uncle! God saves you!; c. negative and pessimistic
9. Scrooge asked his nephew what reason he had to be merry for he was poor enough.
10. a. was a poor but good looking boy.
    c. was excited about Christmas.
    e. was bold enough to challenge his uncle.
11. a. True

        b. True
12. a. Oliver Twist
    b. David Copperfield
    c. Nicholas Nickleby
    d. The Old Curiosity Shop

Journey to the Centre of the Earth

1. Hvar; Nedat; Danish
2. down—"rapid descent" / "descended two thousand feet"
3. a distant waterfall
4. his feelings of intense suffering appeared and he lost all hope
5. "Hans was right, that is the dull roaring of a torrent." / "A torrent"
6. a. True
   b. False
7. roaring, rushing and spluttering; onomatopoeia
8. by passing his hand across the rock hoping to find some trace of humidity; No—"Alas! in vain."
9. a. was probably a man living in the mountains.
   b. was probably experienced in finding water.
   d. had not returned with water.
10. 2 4 3 1
11. a. fiction
12. No—it is all molten lava there

To Build a Fire

1. keenly aware of the danger
2. "squatted"
3. twigs from the brush
4. dry feet; wet feet will freeze
5. the old-timer on Sulphur Creek; "appreciating"
6. "Already all sensation had gone out of his feet."
7. c. He had to stop moving to make his heart work.
8. the unprotected tip of the planet
9. a. the extreme coldness
10. it was alive; it wanted to hide away and cover itself up from the fearful cold
11. hands; legs
12. the fire / the fire was a success

Treasure Island

1. he is not going to relate that voyage in detail
2. a. the captain → understood thoroughly his business
   b. the crew → were capable seamen

44

    c. Mr. Arrow → was a drunkard

    d. Barbecue → was the ship's cook

3. hazy eyes; red cheeks
4. He could attend to his work at least passably.
5. Nobody could ever make out where Mr. Arrow got drunk.

    No—it was never solved

6. Mr. Arrow had fallen overboard
7. the crew on the ship
8. b. promote
9. though he kept his old title, he served in a way as mate
10. a. speak to and trust fully
11. "get on with his cooking like someone safe ashore"
12. being brave; bravery is much needed in fighting or in crises on board a pirate ship.

The Falling Star (The War of the Worlds)

1. a falling star
2. b. Albin

    c. Denning

    d. Ogilvy

3. his French windows faced towards Ottershaw; the blind was up
4. hissing; b. onomatopoeia
5. c. foreshadowing
6. Yes—an enormous hole had been made; the sound and gravel had been flung violently in every direction over the heath, forming heaps visible a mile and a half away
7. No—it was almost entirely buried in sand / only part of it was uncovered
8. it was still so hot from its flight through the air
9. its (huge) size and (cylinder) shape
10. "and dimly perceiving even then some evidence of design in its arrival"
11. the falling star; this strangest of all things; another meteorite; the fallen mass; the shooting star; the projectile; a huge cylinder; the mass; the cindery cylinder
12. called the police (multiple answers accepted)

The Big Four

1. ferry/boat
2. c. would move his suitcase form one spot to another.
3. a legacy
4. the ferry's approaching the white cliffs
5. 18 months; No—his wife was with him
6. emotional
7. He had an egg-shaped head and green eyes.
8. the writer's last letter from Argentina had given no hint of his intended voyage
9. a. juxtaposition
10. a consulting detective and a specialist as a Harley Street physician

11. "He had always scoffed at the popular idea of the human bloodhound who assumed wonderful disguises to track criminals, and who paused at every footprint to measure it."; "Hercule Poirot's methods are his own."
12. her detective novels

Hope

1. the thing with feathers
2. b. a metaphor
3. "And never stops at all,"
4. c. polysyndeton
5. abash it
6. the sound/tune of hope
7. "I've heard it in the chilliest land,
   And on the strangest sea,"
8. No—"Yes, never, in extremity,
   It asked a crumb of me."
9. b. to lift up spirits
10. anaphora
11. old age / weaknesses of old age (multiple answers accepted)
12. a. optimistic

The Great Gatsby

1. music
2. moths
3. d. dancing
4. Yes—
   Rolls-Royce: bearing parties to and from the city between nine in the morning and long past midnight
   Station wagon: meeting all the trains
5. mops, scrubbing-brushes, hammers, garden-shears;
   the guests
6. left at the back door in a pyramid of pulpless halves, juice
7. No—a machine was used
8. canvas and coloured lights
9. No—they were too young to know one from another
10. "no thin five-piece affair"; "a whole pit full of"
11. 2 3 4 1
12. b. pompous

The Painted Veil

1. Waddington; the amah; Walter
2. b. not many who were attacked by it recovered from it.

    c. people died so fast that it was scarcely possible to bury them.

    d. in some houses, everyone died.

3. Yes—there were gods from abandoned temples placed in the streets, and offerings were laid before gods and sacrifices made

4. riot; arson

5. the officer demurred at entering a stricken house

6. "It was very well to say . . ."

7. a. True

    b. False

8. hated; pity

9. Waddington → might be able to help Kitty go home

    Walter (Kitty's husband) → might help if Kitty knelt before him

    Kitty's mother → wanted to get rid of Kitty

    Charlie → had humiliated Kitty

10. b. juxtaposition

11. Kitty knew what he would say if she suddenly appeared before him / Charlie would find it difficult to find words that sounded well / Charlie might humiliate her again

12. c. serious

Les Misérables

1. a. False

    b. True

2. c. it made Jean Valjean shiver.

3. simile; allusion

4. "dropped from his tiptoes to his feet"

5. 4 3 1 2

6. Yes—the noise of the rusty hinge had wakened nobody

7. c. emphasise that Jean Valjean stayed calm despite his fear.

8. He had reached the bed of the bishop sooner than he thought.

9. it was night-time / dark

10. she—nature; which—the bishop's hand

11. For nearly a half hour, a great cloud had been darkening the sky and it broke to let a ray of moonlight to light up the bishop's face.

12. "The souls of the upright in sleep have vision of a mysterious heaven."

The Time Machine

1. somewhere

2. "insensible"

3. a. the sea

4. "of decadent humanity"

5. slower; "the night and day flapped slower and slower."

6. No—it says "he passed like a flash"

7. a. False

       b. True
8. The machine had started from the south-west corner of the laboratory but had come to rest in the north-west.
9. a. had hands and dials to control the time
       c. had come to rest against a wall
       d. had been carried by the Morlocks
10. think/reason; walk easily/properly
11. a. newspaper
12. science fiction

Twenty Thousand Leagues Under the Sea

1. excited; useless
2. c. the writer could not see well.
3. a thick mat
4. No—there was no trace of window or door
5. Yes—"in spite of his own great height"
6. "dense darkness"
7. the electric light
8. Ned Land had a knife in hand.
9. "but we are still in the dark about ourselves"
10. a. imperturbable
      b. inconsiderate
      c. unprofessional
      d. disconnected
11. No—"I could not guess."
12. The first stranger   → b. had more prominent physical attributes.
                          → d. was probably a Frenchman.
    The second stranger → a. looked confident and calm.
                          → c. looked energetic and courageous.
                          → e. deserves a more detailed description.

The Open Window

1. French window
2. a. something very sad
3. Mr. Sappleton, Mrs. Sappleton's two young brothers and a little brown spaniel
4. They were all engulfed in a treacherous piece of bog and their bodies were never recovered.
5. "Here the child's voice lost its self-possessed note and became falteringly human."
6. c. between sunset and darkness.
7. irritated
8. it was a relief to him; he could stop listening to the young girl's horrifying story
9. they had been walking through mud and marshes
10. a. despair / desperateness
      b. partiality / partialness

    c. consciousness

    d. tragedy / tragicness

11. No—Mrs. Sappleton's eyes were constantly straying past Frampton to the open window and the lawn beyond / she yawned

12. a. he meant to show understanding of what the niece had said before about her aunt's delusion.

Search for Mr. Hyde

1. unmarried; bachelor house
2. b. working in his business room before retiring to bed
3. the safe
4. a. False

    b. True

5. a few small sums to the members of the doctor's household
6. No—he sat down with a clouded brow to study the contents of the document, the document had long been his eyesore, and the will was described as "the obnoxious paper"
7. c. metonymy
8. Mr. Lanyon might be able to shed some light on Jekyll's mental state of mind.
9. Yes—he had a butler and he drank wine
10. older; with a shock of hair prematurely white
11. b. the coming of a series of mysterious events
12. someone who has a two-sided personality—a personality alternating between good and evil